by

DOREEN RAMSAY

The Bard of Be'minster

Drawings

by

ANTON BANTOCK

First published 2002 by Doreen Ramsay and

www.malago.org.uk

Second imprint published in 2006 by Broadcast Books
84 Whiteladies Road, Bristol, BS8 2QP
www.broadcastbooks.co.uk.
For order enquiries telephone (0117) 923 8891
or e-mail *catherine@broadcastbooks.co.uk*.

ISBN 978-1-874092-56-8

Royalties from the sale of this book will go to Anton Bantock's
educational charity, the University of Withywood
(www.universityofwithywood.org.uk), and to
the charity *Breakthrough Breast Cancer*,
in memory of our daughter, Lesley Ramsay.

Design and layout by Malago Press and Print Services
(0117) 964 3106 *andrec@andrec.plus.com*

Contents

Down Be'minster

Introduction

IN 1997, on a visit to Bristol Central Library, I saw a notice from the 'Bristol Literature Development Project' asking for people who had 'crossed water to settle in Bristol' to send in their stories. The organisers were, of course, wanting to hear about the experiences of immigrants for a book they were compiling, but the wording struck a bizarre chord with me ...

Water divides the City of Bristol in two, and we cross it every day to and from our respective halves. There has always been a friendly (and sometimes passionate) rivalry between 'North' and 'South', so that evening I put pen to paper and wrote my first ever poem - *The Girt Divide* - which I submitted to *Malago*, a local history magazine published by the Malago Society. They accepted it and asked if I would write in a similar vein about the peculiar charms of shopping 'down Bedminster'.

The request coincided with the closure of Bryan's shell-fish shop, well known throughout the city and the last remaining pre-war East Street establishment. Its demise was the final nail in 'old' Be'minster's coffin and though I'm still not sure if 'old' Bedminster was what the *Malago* magazine wanted, that's what I wrote about in *Down Be'minster* and that's what they published.

A lady unknown to me, who was living in Redcliffe, enjoyed the poem enough to send a copy of it to the Editor of the new *Bristol Times* nostalgia supplement of the *Evening Post* who also published it. So - keeping my fingers crossed - I sent *The Girt Divide* along to them - and they published that too.

When I wrote the pieces, I knew the views I'd expressed were those shared by 'locals', always having been one myself, but I wasn't prepared for the favourable response they got from readers in other parts of the city. Yet I should have known better.

East Street was once a thriving shopping centre known to generations of Bristolians. My own mother, when a child in the 1920s, had regularly been taken there from Hotwells to shop. And in later times, when buses ran to East Street direct from Kingswood, Hanham, Clifton and Redland, and Bedminster had its own railway station, access was easy, goods were cheap and shoppers expected and got good value for money.

The *Bristol Times* dubbed me 'The Bard of Bemmie' and asked me for more poems along the same lines. From then on I could be found loitering with intent 'down Be'minster' with me ear-'ole cocked and me notebook at the ready ...

Doreen Ramsay

THE GIRT DIVIDE

If you're bent on settlin' in Bristol
Then best get it right from the start,
'Cos though it's a beautiful city,
You gotta live in the right part.

We'm split in two by a river, like?
Through the middle - from East to West?
And a stranger might choose the North side,
Not knowing the South side was best.

You'm already half-way to Weston
If you lives on our side of town.
Then there's Portishead and Clevedon -
Not to mention old Brean Down.

The Mendips and Cheddar Gorge is ours
'Cos really we'm Somerset, see?
But on the North side they'm Gloucester,
(With sod-all, between you and me).

And what do THEY know about football?
Bristol Rovers? Call that a team?
Don't make I laugh, we got City.
THE ROBINS. THE REDS. They'm the CREAM.

Where was it you said you did come from?
What? OUR Wells? Or where WELSH is spoke ...?
The outskirts might suit you best, then,
And I'd recommend Bradley Stoke.

DOWN BE'MINSTER

Tain't the same down Be'minster
Since the Cockle Shop shut their door.
You can't get mussels, winkles, whelks
Or toe-rag any more.
And don't dare tell I 'there's ASDAL'
Or you'll get the length of my tongue.
'Cos everything changed when WILLS's went
And ASDAL decided to come.

In the old days we had REAL shops,
What sold proper food an' stuff,
Like chittlin', tripe and pigs trotters
And faggots and peas. And snuff.
Yer taste-buds started a-tinglin'
From the London Inn on down -
(Much to the envy of THAT lot
Out the OTHER END of town).

We even had MARKS & SPENCERS once,
LITTLEWOODS, BRITISH HOME STORES.
All we got left now is WOOLWORTHS
And they ain't the same as before.
Then there was HOME & COLONIAL,
THE MAYPOLE and DAVID GREIGS.
We was spoilt for choice for groceries,
Cooked ham, bacon and eggs.

RAYWARDS sold broken biscuits cheap
And perfect 'uns straight from the tin.
But nowadays you pays top whack
Whatever condition they'm in.
Shops specialised in they days, see?
Took a pride in their knowledge of trade.
And the customers was always right
No matter how little they'd paid.

There was three gents' tailors on the go
And for the ladies 'hote corchor'
From EVE's and WESTON's and ROLLO's
And bleedin' shoe shops galore.
You had to fight to get inside
When Bonus Week hit the town -
Like MILES's when their Club paid out,
Or the PROVIDENT man came round.

I could chat about it for hours
But I can see you'm in a rush
To get inside that superstore
And give yer trolley a push.
I'll browse around the Charity Shops
There's plenty of they about,
Since ASDAL decided to come yer
And WILLS's TOBACCO moved out.

ONE ON EVERY CORNER

Before the supermarkets came
And got us in a strop,
We could find just what we wanted
In our little corner shop.

We didn't need to buy in bulk,
'Cos we could always pop
Half-a-dozen times a day
To our little corner shop.

As well as life's necessities
The gossip too we'd cop.
Rumour was rife on local life
In our little corner shop.

And if we hadn't cleared the slate
We'd let our visits drop
And take our trade just up the road
To our OTHER corner shop.

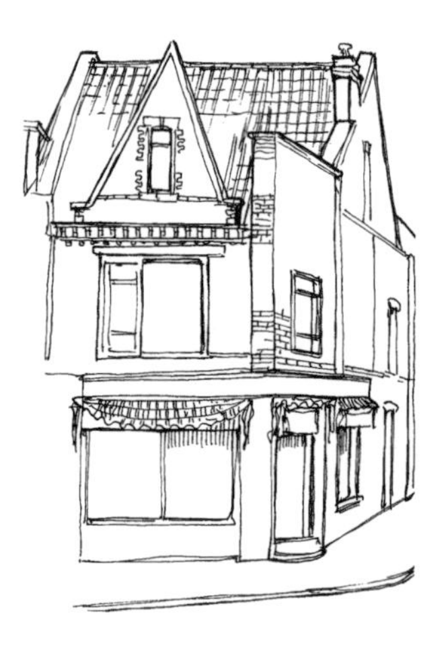

OLD TIMERS

Blimey, Joe - look who it ain't.
It's ol' Fred.
We only said just a minute ago
Thee casn't set foot down Be'minster
Without bumpin' into some bugger thee's know.
So wass doin' down yer, me old cocker?
Don't tell I you'm off to the 'Barley Mow'?
Christ. How many years s'bin goin' in thur?
Thee's coulda bought the place by now.
But you'm looking well on it, babby,
A lot better than me and ol' Joe,
And we bin on the wagon for years.
Healthy livin'? Don't it just go to show.
I've 'ad me 'ip and one knee replaced
Now t'other 'un's startin' to go.
'E's givin' I bleedin' gee-up today,
That's why we'm travellin' so slow.
Still, apart from that and his dicky ticker,
We bain't doin' so bad, be us, Joe?
So have one on we when thee's get thur, Fred,
An' chin-up old son. You'm a long time dead.

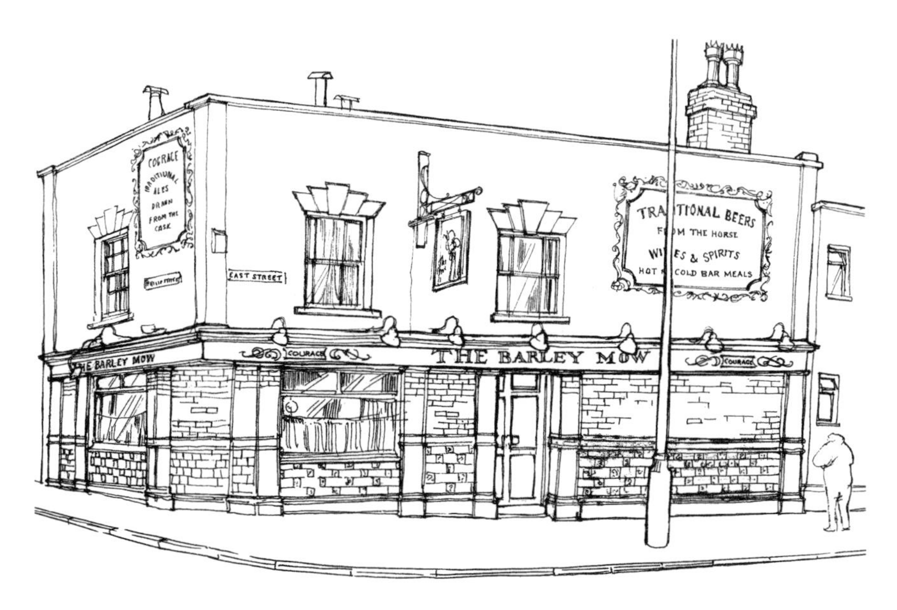

A CHIN-WIPER

Who remembers Pork Butchers shops?
You'm knockin' on a bit, then.
But don't it just make you dribble
Thinking of happy days when
Cholesterol hadn't been heard of,
An' all our meat had some fat,
What we lovingly strained off for drippin'
On our bread, and toast, and all that.
An' faggots bursted with pigs fry
(Chopped liver and lights in a cawl)
An' chittlin' came in three choices,
The fatty, the plaited or mawl.
Every last bit of a porker
You could eat with hardly no waste,
(An no new-fangled additives
That takes away all the taste).
You'd buy a pig's head to make brawn.
Gammon 'ocks glistening with jelly.
An' all the bits in between,
Like trotters, cheeks, tail and belly.
Bath chaps, black pudd'n, sausages,
With no refrigeration,
Furnished the windows years ago
Of Cottles, Modens and Paytons.
They had their fair share of butchers
Out the other end of town too,
But the Pork Purveyors down Bemmy
Took some beatin', I'm telling you.
Nowadays, though, I'd travel
To the ends of the earth and back
If I could tuck into that lot,
Without fear of a 'eart attack.

TEMPUS FUGIT

Another old mucker've pegged it then, Joe.
Jimmie Pringle. He's yer in THE DEATHS.
Don't say what from but, knowin' his form,
T'was most likely shortage of breath.
Forty a day for sixty-odd years.
Quack told'n straight it 'ould end in tears.

Christ Almighty - I don't believe it.
Yer's another 'un right alongside ...
Remember Ted Rawson what lived down Back Lanes?
Well, he bin and upped now and died.
Must 'ave been summat serious, I'd say.
He was always fightin' fit in his day.

BEDMINSTER FUNERAL ESTABLISHMENT
104 East Street Bedminster Bristol 188_
Mr
Dr. to A Hodges
Funeral Featherman Furnishing & Complete Undertakers
Superb Ostrich Plumes Palls Cloaks Velvet for hire
TERMS CASH UNLESS BY SPECIAL ARRANGEMENT 10 PER CENT ON OVERDUE A/C

We seems to 'ave reached a stage in our lives
When frunrals is par for the course ...
So after I've sorted out me black tie
I'll meet thee up the 'White Horse'
And to absent friends we'll drink a toast,
Then I'll cancel the soddin' EVENING POST.

The title of this piece comes from a joke published in the 'Bedminster' book by the Malago Society:

Q. How far is it from the Town Hall to the London Inn?

A. Three miles. (The three shops that made up Miles's store.)

MILES AN' MILES AN' MILES

I've just said goodbye to a tablecloth
That's seen me through thick and thin.
'E cost me three quid down Miles's
When decimalisation came in.
'You won't see cotton like that again,'
I was told when I pulled a jib.
'Your money, madam, will be well-spent.
Sign please.' And it wasn't a fib.
'Cos I'm bound to say what's been said before,
They just don't make 'em like that any more.

I little thought when I left that day
With me cloth neatly parcelled up,
That the time might come, to the housewife's cost,
When Miles's would shut up shop.
And all their commodities fade away
With courteous assistants who used to say,
'Two-and-eleven-three. Will that be all?
Thank you so much.' Then out went the call -
'Sign please.' Bentwood chairs on bare-board floors ...
They just don't make 'em like that any more.

Lingerie. Hosiery. Drapery and such.
Flannelette nightshirts, warm to the touch.
Separate collars with stiffeners and studs
Soaked, scrubbed and boiled in soda and suds.
Haberdashery trays filled to the brim
With buttons, threads and dressmaking trim.
Liberty bodices, whalebone stays,
Where d'you get hold of them, nowadays?
'Sign Please'. Overhead cash flying back and fore.
They just don't make 'em like that any more.

Me tablecloth's seen a few changes, too,
Since the day he left Cannon Street.
Teapot replaced by a bag in a mug.
Milk from a carton, instead of a jug.
Foreign foods and conveniences noshes,
Followed by biological washes
And a tumble-dry instead of a blow.
Small wonder the thing decided to go.
'Resign please.'
He'll be missed, 'cos like Miles's store,
They just don't make 'em like that any more.

PONG SONG

Have you noticed, when strolling through East Street,
There's no smells any more down there?
Apart from they all-day breakfasts, that is,
Coming from YOU-KNOW-WHERE.
But other than that the atmosphere's bland,
Deodorised and hygienic.
And even the shops when you steps inside
Is as sterile as a clinic.

You could cut the air with a knife one time
Down Be'minster on a hot day,
When ozone from the New Cut at low tide
Wafted along the Parade,
To blend with Tannery and tobacco
And burnt roast beans from Carwardines,
While molten sugar from Sweet Factory
Fought with Capper Pass's steam.

The shops theirselves had their own special scent,
Each one was individual;
Like Blackburn's meths, white spirit and wax
Bulk paraffin and linseed oil.
The whiff of Burton's flannel and serge
Evoked quality 'bespoke' suits,
While Hawkins cotton 'Miss Muffet' prints
Spelt country-fresh and cute.

Animal carcasses swinging from hooks
Lined the walls of the butchers' shops,
To be cleavered and chopped before your eyes
(With no additional charge for flies)
And wet fish floundered on marble slab -
Conger-eel, whiting, sprats and dab.
All displayed with no window protection,
Let alone refrigeration.

When your stomach thought that your throat was cut,
You'd head for a cool oasis,
And enter THE PARLOUR if you was flush
To sample Verecchia's ices.
Or standing outside with a penny cone
You had entertainment galore
From the old organ-grinder and monkey
Who played outside Wil-Sam-Mor's.

But although we've been pedestrianised,
Colonnaded and arcaded
With piazzals and seats to 'chew the fat'
That old Bemmy spirit's faded.
'Cos no-one got time to chat any more;
They'm rushing home to the freezer
With pre-packed shrink-wrapped modified food -
But not one nostril-teaser.

HERE, THERE AND EVERYWHERE

Bemmy-bred Bristolians
Don't 'alf put thurselves about.
They'm POPPIN' yer and DAPPIN' thur,
It's a wonder they ain't worn out.

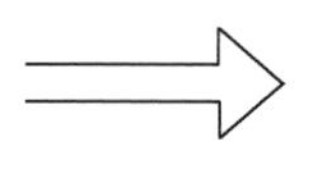

They rushes in all directions
To go where they gotta get.
They never goes straightforward
Least, I never met one yet.

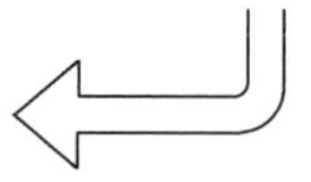

To Broadmead they goes UP
To East Street they goes DOWN.
OUT they goes to Barton 'ill
On the OTHER side of town.

Then it's OVER to Hotwells
And DOWN AROUND the Docks.
ACROSS the Cut to get back 'ome,
Before NIPPIN' round the block.

There's one thing more that puzzles me;
It really makes me frown.
Why do they go DOWN Uphill
But UP the bloomin Downs?

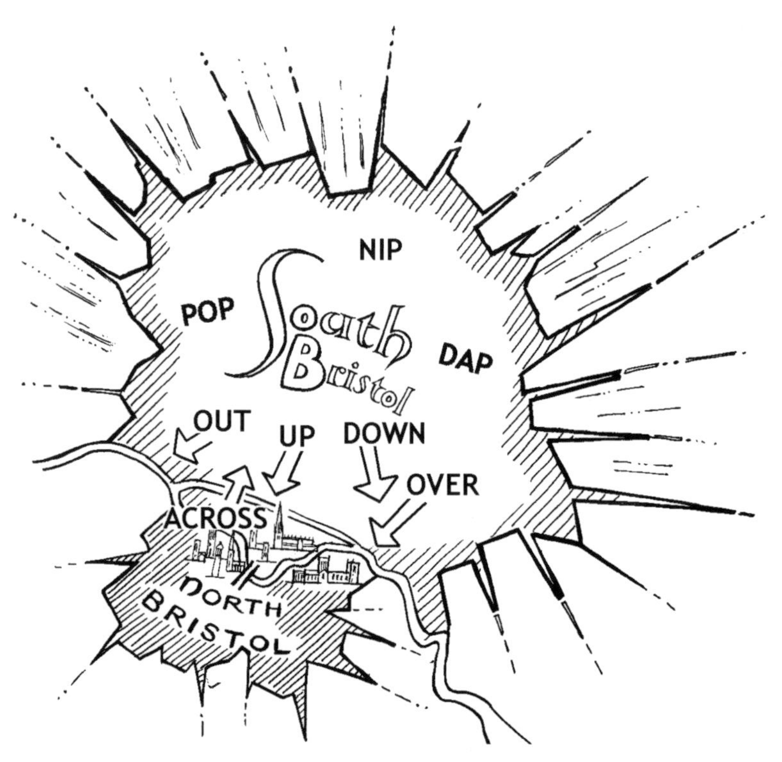

'Protest Poems'

IN 1998 I was doing a bit of 'dappin' about' twice a week to the Bristol Central Library, researching my family history, which had centred around the Docks since the mid-nineteenth century.

My husband's family too had always had close connections with the Shipping Industry and in the 1970s Referendum we had all voted 'NO' to the closure of the commercial port in favour of a Marina.

Now, some thirty years later, the regeneration of our historic harbourside was well under way and the re-vamp of the City Centre about to begin. But every proposal put forward by the Planners was being closely observed and commented on by the dubious citizens of Bristol.

In the following 'protest poems' published in the *Bristol Times* as well as several Local History Magazines, I was expressing not just my own concerns, but those I was hearing around me from passengers on the bus, or reading in the 'Open Lines' pages of the local press.

And I think the many doubts and fears expressed then make interesting reading now - in 2002.

THIRTY YEARS ON

Wass think of it down the docks these days?
Don't bother to answer that.
No doubt, like me, you'm real chuffed to see
Another posh block of flats.

And we'm gettin' a bridge with 'orns on,
Whether we wants one or not.
'He'll be a work of art,' they say,
(Like them unicorns we got).

We ALMOST had that girt glasshouse place.
The sight of 'e made I laugh.
He'd never last like the Colston 'all,
The 'ippodrome or Old Gaff.

And we'm 'avin' a few more pubs and clubs
(What we needs like a 'ole in the 'ead).
There's enough trouble now at closing time,
When everything's done and said.

They skateboards got an arenal, though
(And another on College Green)
So that Referendum was worthwhile
If you chose the Leisure Scheme.

But then, 'VIRTUTE ET INDUSTRIA'
Is what others voted for,
Hoping to keep the old Port alive
Commercially, like before.

When cargo boats, cranes and warehouses
Flanked each side of the harbour
And people was paid a well-earned wage
For seven days hard labour.

But the steamcoal, sand and timber wharves,
Dockers and trading ships' masts,
Are gone now for good. Just like driftwood,
They've sailed away with the past.

But there's some who can still remember
Stacked quays and barges and tugs.
The 'aulin' and 'andlin' and dredgin'
That made up Bristol's life-blood.

It might have been dirty and smelly then,
This proud mercantile city,
But no-one had time to stand and stare,
Or care if the place looked pretty.

Following first reportings of BEAUFORT HOMES' high-rise developments southside of the harbour adjacent to MARITIME MUSEUM (known now as 'The Point') and northside at the junction of Hotwell Road and Jacobs Wells Road on what was Graham's Timber Yard ...

HIDDEN TREASURES

When Hitler finished with Bristol
(Havin' blitzed our heritage down)
The City Planners took over
And re-vamped the centre of town.

At first we thought it was lovely;
A clean sweep, fresh start, and all that,
But when they multi-storeys went up,
We preferred it when it was FLAT.

For years we kept on complaining
'Cos so many lovely church spires
Was blocked out by concrete boxes
That kept getting 'igher 'n 'igher.

But did they listen? Of course not.
They'm still building landscape blots.
Other towns displays what they got.
We'm 'ell-bent on hidin' the lot.

Clifton Wood's gonna disappear
Behind some MORE luxury flats.
(So make the most of Cabot Tower
Before they obliterates THAT.)

And what about our Cathedral?
They've spent millions on College Green
To give'n a worthy setting,
But at the back he's being SCREENED.

Overshadowed by steel and glass -
Just like them churches in the past.
They Planners haven't got a clue.
'Cos they don't listen to me and you.

The family firm of Verecchia (pronounced 'Vereeshal' by Bristolians) was synonymous with ice-cream, particularly in South Bristol. Whereas the reasoning behind 'they 'orns' on PERO'S BRIDGE still remains a mystery ...

THAT 'ORNED BRIDGE

I'd heard a lot about the thing
And none of it was good,
So I went along to see'n for meself.
But the minute I set eyes on'n
A lump come to my throat.
I knew at once what 'e was all about.
They 'orns ain't really 'orns at all.
The medial been having us on.
They'm ice-cream cones from Vereeshals,
Who've now shut-up shop and gone,
After some seventy mouth-waterin' years
Of serving Bristolians so well.
(I read it in the *Bristol Times*
What prints the truth - and some real good rhymes)

Now a friend of our Council's come up trumps,
By floating that lovely concrete lump
With bridge and cornets sitting on top
(Minus Vereeshal's vanilla dollup)
To remind us all of what we've lost
And to pay due homage, no matter the cost,
To ice-cream parlours and travellin' vans
From generations of lickin' fans.
So next time you'm walking out and about
St. Augustine's Reach, stop a while and shout,
'THANK YOU, VEREESHAL'S, FOR BRINGING ME
DELICIOUS ICE-CREAM FROM ITALY!'

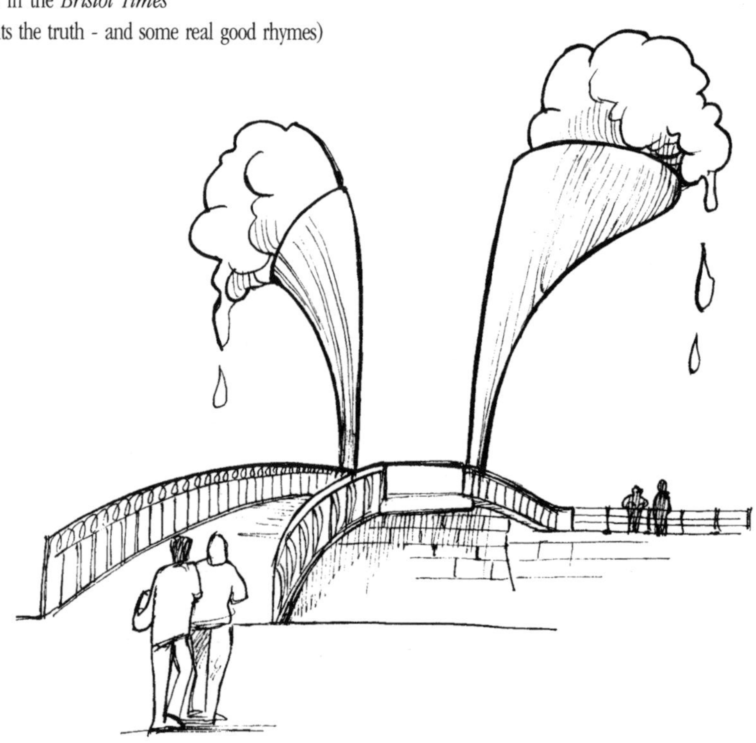

One minute he was there. The next he was gone. Replaced by a pile of rubble and some hazard cones. I felt compelled to take up his case.

MUTINY ON THE BRIDGE HEAD

He've had it up to his eyeballs,
So Neptune's gone off in a huff.
He's sick of the diggin 'n' drillin',
They cones, the diversions and dust.
He don't feel a CONCRETE ocean
Befits a God of the Sea,
Especially as they'm layin' it
Where his harbour used to be.

When first they filled the Centre in
He had his back to it all,
And faced down the Froom quite happy,
Till some bright spark had the gall
To turn'n round the other way
And landward-look day after day,
Surrounded by snarling motor cars,
Like one of they stags at bay.

He did his best to grace the place
But a Sea-God's got his pride,
And he wasn't too pleased about
That 'orned bridge up his backside.
But the final straw, without a doubt,
Was the talk of WATER FEATURES.
Piddlin' fountains doomed to drought
Incensed the mythical creature.

'You can't expect the likes of me
To labour with squirts like that,'
He told 'em round the Council House
An' turned the job down flat.
'The ebb and flow of fountains
To King of the Waves ain't cricket.'
And surrendering his TRIDENT -
He told 'em where to stick it.

As if Bristolians didn't have enough to be going on with in 1999 - a certain Tony Towner told us to 'dig up our dead' and re-locate their remains elsewhere as Amos Vale Cemetery was closed to the public henceforth. All hell let loose at that. The 'Evening Post' launched a 'SAVE OUR CEMETERY CAMPAIGN' and ARNOS VALE ARMY was formed.

At the same time some family papers came into my possession and amongst them was a tiny envelope, addressed in my long-deceased grandfather's handwriting as follows: 'the papers to open the grave of Mrs Annie Clutterbuck, Arnos Vale, Bristol.' It was the receipt for a plot purchased there in 1923, so I decided to put his weight behind the protests, too.

WHO GOES THERE ...

If our Granfer knew what was going on
Out there at Arnos Vale,
He'd rise up through them brambles and weeds
And give that Towner 'ell.
'Cos he didn't pay four pounds fifteen,
Back in Nineteen-twenty-three
For a grass grave and a 'eadstone
To be seized by the likes of 'e.

When he bought that plot our Granfer thought
It was there for posterity.
God knows he didn't own much else;
Few did in them days, see?
But that's where Gran was laid to rest,
Joined by Granfer in 'Forty-five,
And their two names was linked on granite,
To keep their memory alive.

And if Granfer thought for a minute
They was being deprived of their rights,
He'd be down at they gates with a banner
Leading that Cemetery Fight.
He marched for the Docker's Tanner.
He marched with the hungry, too.
He marched to Avonmouth looking for work
And back again, give 'im his due.

But perhaps the word IS getting round
Beneath all that overgrowth ...
And maybe, after the gates is locked
And the watchkeepers have gone home,
Another army is forming
(Led by our Granfer, of course)
Who'll be waiting outside them OTHER gates
For traitors who DARES to cross.

As mentioned earlier, my family history is bound up with the City Docks and my Grandfather looms large throughout as a colourful character who was not backwards in coming forward when anything upset him. So I thought I'd give him the final word in this section.

ODE TO THE BAD OLD DAYS

(and the demise of Georges Brewery)

Granfer lived on the WATERFRONT,
Not far from that Millionaires' Row,
(When Poole's Wharf was still a coal yard,
Before the Sand & Gravel Co.).
And though Granf didn't have a lot -
No cabin-cruiser, skiff or yacht -
Still he managed to keep afloat
Thanks to the Mardyke Ferry Boat.

Daily for a penny each way,
He'd be rowed across the harbour,
Hoping a ship from the Baltic
Would provide a few hours labour.
Running deal on shoulder to shore
For May & Hassel's timber store.
While others made for Mardons, Wills, Robs,
Steady, well-paid, pensionable jobs.

Granfer had no guaranteed work
His skills were the casual sort,
When dock-workers picked at random
Were two-a-penny around the port.
Half his life on the water he spent
Looking for means to pay the rent.
Then week-ends, through all winds and weather,
He'd sail into 'The Plume of Feathers'.

When his slate was full up there,
He'd head on down towards 'The Bear'
And if the landlord called Eight Bells
He's mosey back along Hotwells
Seeking different ports of call
Who might not know his wherewithal.
When flush he'd settle up his bills.
Cock-a-snoot at Mardons, Robs, Wills.

He'd get a nasty shock today
If he strolled round the waterway.
Boatyards, timber wharves, labour-force gone.
Old quays and jetties built upon.
Mardons, Robs, Wills's no longer there.
And, if he was a millionaire,
The Bear, the Plume and the Mardyke too,
Still wouldn't serve him Georges Home Brewed.

CASTLE STREET REMEMBERED

'Remember Castle Street?' they say.
Wine Street and Mary-le-Port ...
Trips by tram on Saturday nights
To that magical shopping resort.

Where buskers with hurdy-gurdies played
And barrow-boys shouted their wares
And flappers and dandies paraded
In search of a 'grand affair'.

While canny housewives, light of purse,
Kept an eye on the butchers' shops
Knowing full-well the price would drop
Before the night's trading had stopped.

Then some, with a quid or two to spend
On a frock for the Folk House Hop,
Window-gazed outside Baker-Baker's
And Jones's ... or Goss's Silk Shop ...

Round at the REGENT the wurlitzer rose,
Enthralling the couples who'd 'clicked'
Outside the flashiest 'flea-pit' in town
For an up-to-date Hollywood 'flick'.

While cockles and mussels alive-alive-o,
Pigs trotters and pinky-fruit frails
Were happily stowed on the homeward trams
To Bedminster ... or ... Hotwells ...

Remember Castle Street, they sigh.
Wine Street and Mary-le-Port ...
Of course I do, but the scene I knew
Was of a different sort.

Where only the Co-op reigned supreme
Over the bombed sites round Castle Green,
For World War Two had come between
Memories of how it used to be.

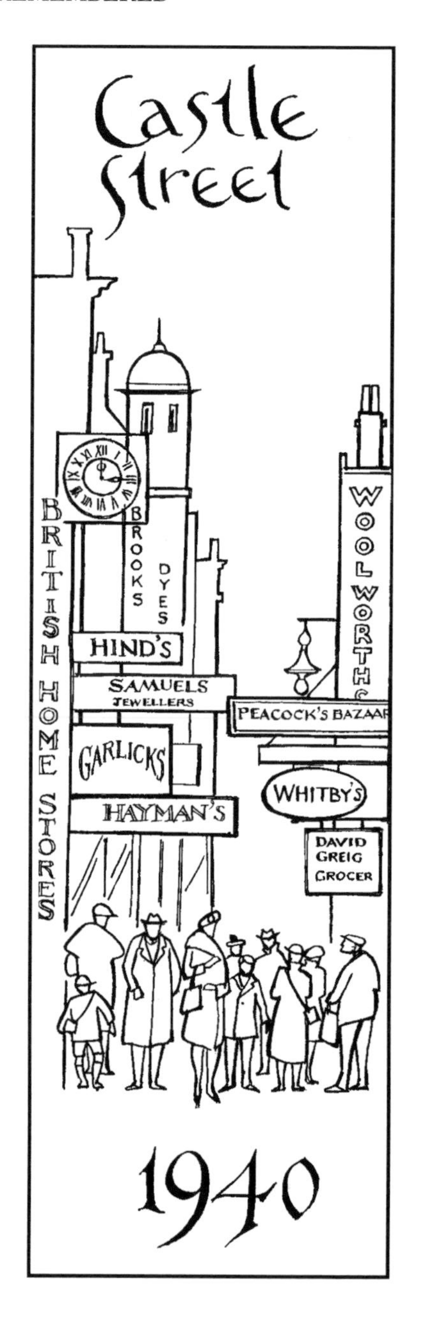

GOOD FRIDAY

Darkest of days in any event -
When RELIGION ruled and churches filled
With faithful summoned by noonday bell.
Good Friday.

Always then, from twelve till three,
A shroud of silence, guilt, betrayal
Settled on all who did not heed
Good Friday.

Anticipation. Apprehension.
'Wash not in the Saviours's blood'
Idled hands through superstition,
Each Good Friday.

Easter-egg-and-hot-cross-bun-less,
Darkly dawned one wartime day.
Crucifixion all around them
That Good Friday.

April night-sky bright and clear,
Full moon and a million stars
Aided enemy planes to blitz,
One Good Friday.

Nineteen-hundred-and-forty-one -
Huddled together in fear -
They prayed to the ONE
Whose suffering was done
On Good Friday.

THEY ALSO SERVED

Dedicated to all the 'little men' of the Fighting Forties.

I didn't spend much time with men
Because, before the age of ten,
They were so few and far between,
Glimpsed briefly on a silver screen
As part of Gaumont-Pathé News.
Marching off, no time to lose.
Brave deeds to do, a war to win,
But always with a cheery grin.
Though just a boy, I longed to be
Allowed to fight for my country.
Instead, I had to be content
With balaclava, kindly lent,
And gun torn from a bomb-site tree
That led to certain victory.
Home Front battlefields held no fear
For 'Spitfire pilot' or 'Frigateer'.
All fights were fought with hero's pluck
(And more than a fair share of luck).
So, when my grandson asks of me
In which I served? I say, 'ALL THREE'.

Although I grew up in what had been a built-up part of the city, I had the luck to be surrounded by the bombed site prairies of blitzed Bristol and they proved a great playground - especially in the BIG FREEZE of 1947 when the 'battle fields' and 'Wild West' turned overnight into THE ALPS.

Shortly afterwards, though, the post-war rebuilding programme began and the adventure was over.

SEARCHLIGHTS OVER BEMMY

Prologue to my three-act play of the same name, written and staged to mark the 50th anniversary of the Good Friday blitz on Bedminster.

In November nineteen-forty,
Bristol went to war.
We lost the City Centre -
You've heard all that before.

But nothing very much is said
About OUR bit of town;
The bit that runs from Redcliffe Hill
And up to Bemmy Down.

Yet, back in nineteen-forty-one,
Hitler did his best
To wipe out our bit of Bristol,
When he'd finished with the rest.

That tightly-packed community
Was shaken to its core
By the loss of homes and families,
The like not seen before.

But courage wasn't only found
Inside a uniform,
All those Bedminster civilians too,
Stood up to the storm.

Our local men and women
Then reached the very height
Of courage and endurance
In the front line of the fight.

As cheerfully and bravely
They answered to the call
And once they were remembered
In St. Dunstan's Parish Hall.

It was just a little tribute,
A walk down Memory Lane,
Recalling names and places
That we'd never see again.

But the thing that KEPT emerging
After fifty peaceful years,
Was the comradeship and laughter
That helped them through their tears.

So that's what we'll look back on
From this Third Millennium.
We'll wallow in nostalgia
And have a bit of fun.

The wireless was our window on the world and newscaster Alvar Lidell became one of the family. The wireless belted out our favourite songs, cheered us up with shows like ITMA, MONDAY NIGHT AT EIGHT, HAPPIDROME, etc., and sent us to bed petrified with the blood-curdling tales of Valentine Dyall - 'THE MAN IN BLACK'. Our greatest escape, of course, was the cinema and the glamour of Hollywood. I used all of the above as a backdrop to my play - and now it's 'CURTAIN UP' on some ...

LIGHT BYTES FROM DARK DAYS

We had *Sister Suzie Knitting Socks for Soldiers*
And Mother tuned to tips on 'Kitchen Front'.
Poor Granfer tried his best to Dig for Victory
While Father did his Air Raid Warden stunt.

Kids *Praised the Lord and Passed the Ammunition*
As they acted out their war on debris sites -
Challenging the Hun - shooting Hitler up the bum,
With a hoarse reminder, 'Careless Talk Costs Lives.'

Tommy Handley entertained us on the wireless,
I*t's* ***T****hat* ***M****an* ***A****gain* the Nation's favourite show.
Don't forget the Diver, Colonel Chinstrap, Mona Lott,
And T.T.F.N. meant 'it's time to go'.

Betty Grable flounced her way through every picture.
Deanna Durbin warbled like a thrush.
Bette Davis, Barbara Stanwick,
Puffed their way through endless packets,
But Gene Autrey ruled the week-end Sixpenny Rush.

Mardons, Robs and Wills's sang their socks off
With *Workers' Playtime* on the factory floor.
They let it rip with Vera, Glen Miller, Dinah Shore
And tried to Cheer Our Lads Up - *Bless 'em all.*

Then *Anchors Aweigh, When The Saints Came Marching In*
With the *Boogie-Woogie Bugle Boy* in tow.
On a Wing and a Prayer, Yanks were here from *Over There*
And just what went on then *You'll Never Know ...*

YANKED

(to the tune of *The Isle of Capri*)

'Twas on the Bridgwater Road that she met him,
On the outskirts of Bedminster Down.
She asked 'Have you got any gum, chum?'
He said 'Sure, if you'll show me around.'

She suggested a stroll to the Centre
But she couldn't get him to agree.
Then when he promised her nylons,
She said 'Yes' to the 'Roadhouse Mile 3'.

'Twas on the Bridgwater Road that he taught her
Things she'd never experienced before.
And by the end of that evening
She'd been jitter-bugged all round the floor.

A WARTIME ROMANCE

(and they said it wouldn't last)

It all began with a parcel of fags
Sent by a kind-hearted WREN
To her brother's mate serving in Norway,
One of our 'fighting men'.
'I don't know if you'll remember me,'
Wrote Six-Five-Four-Six-Seven ...
'The last time we met we were only kids -
Just about eleven.'
Now One-Four-Four-O-Five-Five-Three
Straightened his Red Beret,
And like any good Paratrooper would,
Wrote back without delay.
'Thanks for the 100 Players Weights.
Of course I remember you well ...
Playing hopscotch on the pavement
When I rang your Bertie's bell.
Perhaps we'll meet again someday
When the lights go on after the war?'
'I don't mind if we do,' thought the WREN,
And sent him 100 more.

Now Paratrooper Ted Carrington
Sipped at his ration of beer
Beside a Norwegian fjord and thought,
'I'm onto a winner here.
If I was to play my cards right,
P'raps down Victoria Park.
I could land up in bed with a WREN
And get up to a lark.'
When his Embarkation Leave came through
He duly got in touch
With Violet Philpotts,
Though in truth, he DIDN'T remember her much.
'My train's arriving at midnight,' he wired.
'Be ready and waiting my sweet
At Bedminster Railway Station.'
Young Violet was swept off her feet.
She'd only just put her curlers in,
Her hair was still wringing wet,
But she covered it up with a turban
And off to her destiny set.

It was just like *Brief Encounter*
When the couple came face to face,
And Ted knew Vi was the one for him
When she offered to carry his case.
He popped it out half-an-hour later
When the kissing and cuddling was through,
'Let's get married,' he said,
'Cos once we're wed,
I'll get an Allowance for TWO.'

Five days later Vi stood at the altar,
A trembling virgin in white.
'I paid two guineas for this,' hissed the groom,
'So you'd better be worth it tonight.'
Before the CONSUMMATION though,
The wedding breakfast took place
At St. Dunstan's church hall in Bedminster
(Thanks to His Majesty's Grace).
Trifles sneaked out from the Officers' Mess
At the BMH on the Downs
To a jeep commandeered from the Army
And secreted away in the grounds.
Then posthaste to a house down Luckwell Road
To dig up the Groom's back yard
For surplus tinned NAAFI provisions -
By now a bit rusty and scarred.
But the guests had seen nothing like it,
Such luxuries were scare due to war.
'Best knock it back quick,'
Warned the bride and the groom,
'The Scouts is due in here at four.'

On the first day of March 1946 -
If you'd been around there that day,
You'd have seen a motley procession
Marching down Parson Street way,
Still in their wedding finery,
And bearing the left-over food
To carry on partying down Marksbury Road
While they were still 'In The Mood'.

'Where are we spending our wedding night?'
The blushing bride wanted to know.
'Thanks to that Special Licence,' hedged Ted,
'I'm a little bit short of dough.
But fret you not, my precious -
You'll climb the stairway to heaven
When I gets you to Little Paradise.
We've got our Gran's place till Eleven.'
Thirteen pints later that evening,
Poor Vi heaved her groom into bed.
She looked at him snoring beside her,
'That's his first promise broken,' she said.
'What on earth have I done,' she pondered,
Twisting the little gold band
That Our Hero - just a few hours before -
Had placed on her trembling hand.
'Marry in haste,' her mother had warned,
'Repent at leisure, they say.'
But Vi never dreamed she'd be doing just that
Till their Golden Wedding Day.

I attended the Bedminster Tabernacle in Palmyra Road for the final two years of the war. I was only 9-10 years old at the time.

HALF-WAY UP PALMYRA

I blames my fame on the BAPTISTS.
They spawned my dramatic flair,
'Cos at Tabernacle on Sundays
I'd sit rooted to my chair
As speakers took to the pulpit
And preached the Word of the Lord
With an animated fervour
I'd never encountered before.

Then Superintendent Faithful,
Silver-suited and wax-moustached,
Would lead us into the final hymn
And we'd all raise the roof, unabashed.
I was a *Sunbeam for Jesus*
I was *H A P P Y.*
But before I joined they Baptists
I was really rather shy.

Especially one - Pastor Moody -
Rotund of stature and voice.
He was a real Bible Basher
Urging us all to rejoice.
While underneath the pulpit
The River Jordan flowed
And sinners who chose to be baptised
Held their noses and closed their eyes
As the Pastor dunked 'em in full length
Calling on God to give'n the strength.

'They Baptists' certainly made an impression on me because 45 years later it was The Tabernacle, and the people who worshipped and/or lived in its vicinity, who furnished all the characters and a large part of the plot of both 'Searchlights' and 'War and Peace over Bemmy', together with Ted Hill's 'Tell your Mother there's a War on', with the permission of the Malago Society.

A New Millennium Miscellany

WITHOUT any explanation, both the *Evening Post*, which had once had a poetry page, and the *Bristol Times*, which had encouraged me to submit my work, stopped publishing verse, and so, come 2000, I was left with a collection of new dialect pieces which were going nowhere.

Then, half-way through the year, a friend invited me to read some of my work to the 'Memories of Bedminster' Group, which I was very happy to do as they had generously published several of my pieces on local life in their *Remember Bedminster* magazine. As a result, invitations from other clubs followed thick and fast and the 'Bard of Bemmie' turned 'performance poet' with 'supply' struggling to keep up with 'demand'.

Some of the following monologues have been published, others only performed.

A letter attacking the Bristolian accent appeared in the 'Evening Post' and readers were swift to retaliate (one way or the other). This was my published contribution to the debate - and the Paper's final word on the subject ... at least for the time being.

A BEE IN ME BONNET

I've got a bee in me bonnet
That's been buzzin' about for years.
It concerns our Bristol accent
And the way that outsiders jeers.
There's plenty of 'em lives yer, too,
Who groans and goes all toffee-nosed
When they 'ears us on the medial
Expoundin' our pleasures and woes.
But I'll tell thee summat, lover,
There's many speaks worse than we do.
Just listen to 'em on telly
An' you'll find what I says is true.

Take *The Bill* and they *Eastenders*
Their vowels is all over the plice.
Their 'RINE IN SPINE FAWS ON THE PLINE'
And of haitches there AIN'T A TRICE.
It's BRUVVA, MUVVA and FAVVA,
Not our kid, our Mal, or our Dad.
And as for north of the Border -
Well - their lingo is barkin' mad.
But you never 'ears a word of abuse
Over the way THEY talks.
In fact they'm paid a very good wage
For entertainin' folks.
The Scotch, they Welsh and the Irish
Gets their fair share of viewin' space,
And as for they Australian soaps,
They'm all over the blinkin' place.

But though they films that *Casualty* yer
Because the scenery's pretty,
You don't 'ear patients from Bristol
Being treated in 'Holby City'.
But they who laughs last laughs longest.
Mark my words - the right time will come
For us to market 'BRISTOLESE'
Without the world pokin' fun.
So keep on addin' that Bristol 'L'
An' stretchin' they West Country 'Rs'
Forget word endin's, 'cos someday
That DIALECT CROWN will be ours.

The press is well-supplied with letters of complaint about Bristol's bus service. Yet in 1999 the reporting of a 'TRANSPORT CITY OF EXCELLENCE BID' by the Council was overlooked by everyone - except me.

WELCOME ABOARD

He didn't half have it about him.
He was thumping and banging about,
Pursing his lips and slamming his eyes,
Huffing and puffing and heaving sighs,
Snorting and grunting, having a cuss,
Because he had passengers on his bus
Who'd been waiting half-an-hour or more
To go where they'd never been took before
By a driver who didn't know his way
'Cos the rota'd been changed again that day.
So they let him have it hard and fast
About bus services in the past,
When green double-deckers cruised through town
And timetables never let you down
And conductors helped you all aboard
And charged you fares you could afford,
Not robbed you bline and shook you around
By pulling away 'fore a seat was found.
The young stood up and the old sat down
And one bus took you right across town
Before Old Market was out of bounds
And The Centre redesigned by clowns.
And if you got lost an Inspector knew
Exactly which bus was the one for you.
Now nobody had a bleedin' clue
And couldn't care less, to tell the truth.
'TRANSPORT CENTRE OF EXCELLENCE BID?'
The passengers roared. And the driver did.
United they saw the funny side.
'Have a good day, mate. Thanks for the ride.'

Written after 'Saving Private Ryan' at the 'Showcase' cinema ...

MULTI-PLEXED OFF!

Have you been to the pictures lately?
Well, take my advice and don't go.
They multi-screen jobs is a menace;
Not a bit like the flicks years ago.

We'd queue up for hours in the old days
For a seat in the one-and-nines
And stay put once we got settled
To see the main feature three times.

We'd champ through our Sharps's toffees
Till the National Anthem came round,
Then we was gone like greased-lightning,
Before a drum-roll could sound.

We'd hike it to The Ambassador,
The Town Hall, The Ashton, The Rex.
Now you gotta drive for bloomin' miles
To some Outer Mongolia Complex.

After you've found a parking space,
You heads for the 'dazzledrome'
For your hotdogs, coffee and popcorn.
Talk about 'home from home'.

You've kissed 'goodbye' to a tenner
Before reaching yer blessed seat -
An 'e reclines till you'm laid flat out
With yer 'ead on some stranger's feet.

Then, munchin', crunchin' and slurpin'
You plays trivial pursuits with the screen;
Like guessing how many beans makes five,
But not a film to be seen.

Just when you finds yourself droppin' off,
You'm blasted rudely awake
By that 'surround-a-sound' and you thinks
You'm caught in some full scale earthquake.

It goes on like that for three hours,
Till you finally staggers outside
Stone deaf, with a blinding 'eadache
And facing a three-mile ride ...

Gone is the swish of the curtain.
The lure of the old silver screen.
Usherettes torching you to your seat
And intervals for an ice-cream.

Gone is the Gaumont-Pathé News,
The 'B' films and old Mickey Mouse.
Gone too, though, thank God,
They brass-buttoned twerps
Who LOVED to yell 'SORRY - FULL HOUSE.

A MAIDEN'S VOYAGE

He sat on the strap of my handbag
Just as *Titanic* set sail.
I didn't know him from Adam,
And being a bashful female,
I didn't heave it or tug it,
But decided to let matters bide,
Unaware that we were about to share
A very emotional ride.

The first half was all plain sailing;
I began to enjoy the cruise.
With my handbag safely between us,
I felt I had nothing to lose.
But when the ship hit that iceberg
The whole situation changed.
He started wriggling and writhing
And my bag shot out of my range.

I was all at sea without warning,
Floundering in wave after wave
Of panic and consternation;
But, trying hard to be brave,
I groped about in the darkness
And got more than I'd bargained for,
'Cos next thing I knew, my hand was inside
His carton of freshly popped corn.

That was a shock, believe me;
I hit it all over the floor.
He dived to the rescue like lightning;
Talk about 'Man Overboard'.
As I was the cause of the mishap,
I followed him under the seat,
Not wishing to spoil his evening
By depriving him of a treat.

We heard the passengers screaming,
And the creaks and groans of the boat
Over our heads in the darkness,
As we knelt and fumbled about,
Safe from the perils of the sea,
There on the floor - just him and me -
While the violins played, appropriately,
'Nearer, my God, to Thee. Nearer to Thee.'

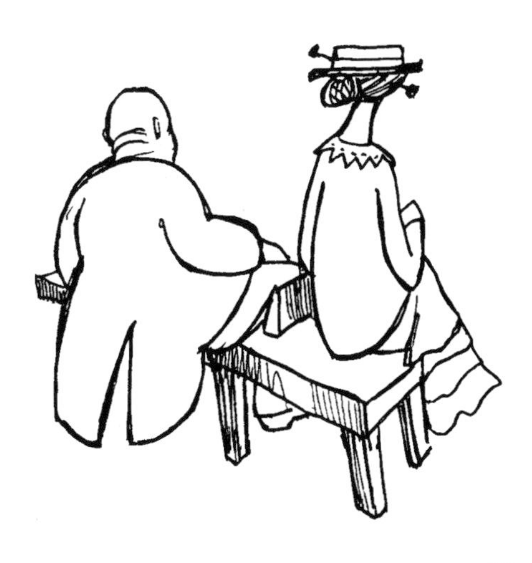

My husband and I had taken our grandchildren to the 'Tropicana' at Weston-super-Mare. While they were enjoying their watersports I was left in charge of a mountain of baggage, which inspired the following ...

WHEN IGNORANCE WAS BLISS

A day trip to Weston ain't what it was;
You goes by car, for a start.
By the time you've finished loading the thing,
You'm having a change of heart.

In goes the table, umbrella and chairs,
Then you starts packing the food.
They expects a three-course picnic now
And you gets in a right old mood.

Remember they carefree outings of old,
By train; when a carrier bag
Held an 'andsome banquet of bread and scrape
Wrapped up in a dampened rag?

And a bottle of water to wash it down,
With Kali if you was 'flush',
Which was gone before yer bum hit the sand
'Cos yer belly was in such a rush?

And if the bloomin' tide had gone out
You didn't sit round and complain,
You'd wade through the mud half-way to Wales
And meet'n back in again.

Course, we didn't have no pollution then,
Just the odd sheep's carcass or two;
And we'd never HEARD of sewage,
And all that how-do-you-do.

The weather was better in them days, too,
The sun shone from morning to night.
And if you got burnt, which you always did,
A calamine dab put you right.

Now you daresn't go out on a decent day
Without smearing Factor Ten
All over yer bits and pieces.
It's hardly worth botherin' then.

'Cos we'm suffering from global warming,
E. Coli bugs in the sand,
Mad cow disease in our sandwiches,
Road-rage and traffic jams.

So it ain't worthwhile goin' to Weston,
Especially as it might rain.
Better stay home and save up all year
For a week's Salmonella in Spain.

Some widely felt views on a certain T.V. Cookery Programme ...

READY - STEADY - YUK

Wass up with all they half-baked meals
They'm dishin' up on telly?
I wonder they're not suffering
With ragin' dysentery.
They can't kid me a leg of lamb
Cooks in twenty minutes flat.
What they calls 'rare' I says is raw,
When oozin' blood an' all that.

And when they do's a bit of fish
They leaves his blinkin' head on.
He lies there gawpin' on the plate
Both glassy eyes wide open.
They haven't got the decency
To cover 'im in batter.
Sometimes I swear he's half-alive
Listenin' to 'em natter.

As for they fancy foreign foods,
Me lips remains sealed on that
(Except to say I wouldn't dare
Put it in front of our cat).
God KNOWS what they'm camouflaging
Under they herbs and spices.
But fish or fowl, it's sure to come
With 'healthy wholegrain rices'.

Can you imagine, years ago,
Settin' in front the old man
A blob of flesh with asparagus
On an empty plate? I can.
'Thee's know what thee could'st do with that,'
Would be his first reaction.
And then the fat would hit the fire
Till he got satisfaction.

Meat, three veg and a hunk of bread
To mop up all the gravy
Would be the order of those days;
No parsley - flat or wavy.
But well-cooked food's unfashionable,
They says it spoils the flavour.
I wish they'd have a power cut
And do us all a favour.

A FAMILY AFFAIR

Father's favourite daughter, Queenie,
Drove her family mad.
'Ideas above her station'
Is what Mother said she had.
And all because she'd married well -
The local Undertaker
(Who Mother hadn't taken to
And nobody could make her).

'The very thought of what he does
Makes my flesh creep,' she'd sigh,
'I've noticed too, that when we meets,
He don't look me in the eye,
But takes me in from head to toe,
As if he was measuring me up.
Rich or poor, he leaves me cold,
I'd rather be hard-up.'

Nevertheless, whenever he called,
Mother would get in a state,
Trying to find an unchipped cup
With matching saucer and plate.
Jam was served in a dish with spoon
And tea poured through a strainer.
He really gave her the jitters;
She couldn't have made that plainer.

'I don't want him telling Queenie
That I've been caught nappin',' she'd say.
'She thinks she's so superior,
And that would make her day.
Bone china or no, she's welcome though,
To Ambrose Chard and his trade.
'Cos every time his hand meets mine
I feels I'm being 'laid'.'

'As long as our Queenie's happy,'
Father told her with pride,
'That's all that matters in my book,
So let others' business bide.'
Mother clattered and clanged about,
Warning, 'I know that I'm right.
He's got a funny look in his eye
That makes me go weak with fright.'

She upped her Penny Policy to tuppence.
Just to make sure
She was fully insured against the odds
Of FATE knocking on her door.
And it did, 'cos Queenie came crying,
'He's left me for another.'
'No need to tell me,' stormed Father,
'He's run off with yer mother.'

Written for M & S Retirement Staff Association ...

MOURNING ST. MICHAEL

I hear Marks & Spencers is going broke -
Which doesn't surprise me at all.
If they spoke to me I could tell 'em straight
The cause of their decline and fall.
And it's nothing to do with their price tags -
St. Michael's stuff never came cheap -
But you used to get value for money,
Provided your pocket was deep.

Now their quality's taken a turn for the worse,
And that 'personal service' has gone.
You don't see nobody walking the floor
To put things back where they was before.
Have you tried to find a matching pair
Of shoes when they'm lying about everywhere?
You'm wearing the left, someone else the right;
Next thing you'm involved in a FOOT-GLOVE fight.

That lingerie Department of theirs beats all,
With brassieres hanging all over the wall,
Which means that the world and his wife can see
If your bust is a forty-four, double-D.
While their knickers is infinitissimall.
And wouldn't keep very much warm at all.

Then there's the husbands all mooning about
In a soporific state
Dreaming of their twelve-stone wives
Languishing in a size 8
Balcony bra and a G-string,
Knowing full-well she'll decide
On a 'Total Control' and full-length briefs,
Which secretly comes as quite a relief,
'Cos they knows they'd find the going tough
If they had to rise to that sort of stuff.

Mind you - I blames them fitting rooms
For a lot of the problems they've got.
All the mirrors inside is distorted,
As though they've come from a REJECT lot.
In front of my looking glass at home
Me body's in perfect condition.
But when I strips off in Marks and Sparks
There's been a transfiguration.
Me hour-glass figure's gone pear-shape
And looks like it's covered in yellow crepe.

I didn't have any trouble before
They introduced cubicles into the store.
If I seen a frock I liked I'd just buy it -
Knowing my fit without having to try it.
'Cos their sizes was more reliable then,
A 12 meant a 12 and 10 meant a 10.
Now I'm straining to get me torso between
What they'd have me believe is a size sixteen.

But I've sussed it out why they'm losing trade.
It's because these days all their clothes are made
By foreigners in Turkey - Morocco - Taiwan
Who keeps sewing the wrong bloomin' labels on.

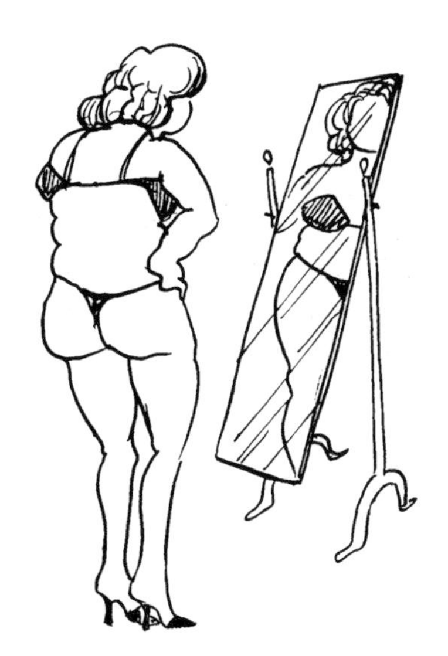

SLEEPING PARTNERS

Clevedon beach on a summer's day.
Fred and me and another pair.
Getting on - but smartly dressed -
They was really enjoying it there.

You could tell they wasn't husband and wife
'Cos they had too much to say.
And he really listened when she spoke
Which proved he was a single bloke.
For husbands don't absorb a word,
Or else pretends they haven't heard,
Until they'm watching *Match of the Day*
Or a politician's having his say.
They'm ready then to pontificate -
'You must be bloody jokin', mate.'

But these was engrossed in each other,
Having a laugh and a joke,
And if there'd been the slightest doubt
About them NOT being married folk,
His next words set the record straight -
'Had your hair done, dear? It's looking great.'

Now how many husbands ever knows
When you haves a perm or wears new clothes?
I could do a 'streak' with me head shaved bald
And I'd get, 'shut the door - it's turning cold'.
I've had my mop dyed blonde, black and red
But if he noticed, he never said.
When prompted once he sighed all peeved,
'Well ... it always looks alright to me.'

I tell you what though, he'd be well-trained
If he had to start courting all over again.
'Cos all the mistakes he's made with me
Would be ironed out for next time, see?
Like that bloke on the beach, he'd pay due heed
To his fancy woman's every need.
If she wanted to talk he'd bend an ear
And tell her, 'that's really interesting, dear',
Instead of interrupting me in full flow
With, 'Sssh. City've scored. That's three in a row.'

But I'd doubt he'd stay conscious long enough
To entertain a new bit of stuff.
Look at'n laid there snortin' and blowin'.
Oi. Wake up Fred - it's time we was goin'.

On seeing Christmas decorations in store shortly after one August Bank Holiday ...

BUT ONCE A YEAR

When Christmas came but once a year
And lasted for only two days,
We had a lot more fun than now
Despite all our old-fashioned ways.
Father would fetch the fowl home,
And after he'd been plucked and drawn
He'd be stuffed both ends by Mother -
That's the fowl, not Father - who'd gone
Off to the pub for his Christmas pint,
While Mother set into the Port.
Only a little tipple, mind,
She wasn't the drinkin' sort.
But she'd be singing *White Christmas*
With Bing on the gramophone,
And when Father rolled in later,
She'd give him *Home Sweet Home*.
We kids 'ould be all a do-dah
As we got our letters to fly
Up the flue to Father Misher,
Hoverin' somewhere in the sky.
He always brought what we wanted,
Which wasn't a lot, you'll agree,
But Christmas morning was magic
And full of festivity.

We'd waited all year for that chicken
And pudd'n with threepenny-bit,
So in we all tucked with gusto,
Our stomachs like bottomless pits.
Christmas night was always party-time,
When the family got together.
Everyone turned up full of good cheer
For a knees-up, whatever the weather.
On Boxing Day it was football
(After cold meat and bubble'n'squeak),
Then round to our Gran's to finish up
Everything THEY couldn't eat.
That was it and all about it,
But the memory lasted all year.
All that lasts now is the debt they'm in,
Where everything's costing so dear.
'Cos every day is Christmas Day -
They lives on the fat of the land;
So they goes overboard at Yuletide
And gets into the credit band.
But however sumptuous their table,
I bet things won't taste 'alf as good
As that little fowl our Father plucked,
Or Ma's 'ome-made Christmas pud.

THE BALLAD OF BILLY AND JOE

I'd like to tell you a story
That an old man once told to me,
About the time he was working
Down the Pit in South Liberty.

A murky grey dawn was breaking
As Joe and his mate, Billy Vine,
Hurried across the Old Black Bridge
That straddled the railway line.

A Goods Train trundling underneath
Belched a cloud of sulphurous steam
Around the pair who lingered there,
Nourishing a run-away dream.

But eight hundred feet below ground
Was where they were destined that day.
Like rats in the dark and the damp,
They'd labour for Colliery pay.

In silence they trudged on to work,
Neither giving a backward look,
Then - 'Christ Almighty,' gasped Billy,
As they drew near to Colliters Brook.

He pointed with shaking finger,
As out of the rushes and reeds,
Crept two fat rats clutching a straw,
An end each between their teeth.

Now rats was two for a penny
In those days, and Joe couldn't see
Why Billy was pale and trembling
As he darted behind a tree.

'One of they rats is a BLACK 'un,'
Hissed Billy with bated breath,
'They what brings pestilence and plague.
Thee's know what I means, THE BLACK DEATH.

Without a further how-d'you do
He picked up a stone lying round,
And aimed it at the evil rat
Which was felled at once to the ground.

Its brown companion stood rooted,
No effort it made to escape;
With whiskers a-twitch it waited,
Staring straight ahead into space.

Slowly Joe beckoned Bill forward,
Whisp'rin, 'Yer, take a look at that.
He 'on't move a step without his mate,
Cos he's as blind as a bat.'

'What to do now?' croaked Billy,
And Joe heard the tears in his voice.
Clearing his own throat he muttered,
'I don't see we got any choice.'

'You'll have to go, my old sonner,'
Gently Joe stroked the rat's head.
No other action was needed,
'Cos the poor thing dropped down stone dead.

'It must have been shock that killed'n,
Or the loss of a real good mate,'
Cogitated the two young men
As they approached the Pithead late.

'I'll tell thee what, Billy,' said Joe,
I've learned a big lesson from that.
In the worst of us there's some good,
Be it Colliery Boss or Black Rat.

'An' a miner's life ain't so bad
If he's got a friend by his side
Who shares a vision of freedom
By 'itchin' a one-way train ride.'

Based on a true story by my grandfather (Parker) who worked down this particular pit at the age of fourteen.

HAPPY AND GLORIOUS

So the Queen won't be coming to Bristol
In her Golden Jubilee Year.
I hope it's nothing to do with the fact
That I wrote to the poor old dear,
And tried to explain how Bristol had changed
Since the last time she visited here.

I warned her not to wait for a bus
Outside Temple Meads (or anywhere else),
'Cos ten to one she'd have to stand
If one EVER arrived from no-man's-land.
I suggested she go by ferry instead
And cruise around to the old Bridgehead.
And p'raps as she chugged under Pero's Bridge
She could cast an eye at they horns on its ridge,
Then with her wealth of historic sense
Tell the rest of us what they represents.

And don't go looking for Neptune, I said,
If you seen where they've stuck'n you'd wish'n dead.
I warned her The Centre Gardens had gone.
Replaced by a wobbly-cobbly prom,
With timber decking you skidded along,
And fountains and lights (more off than on).
It's a real life Extreme Adventure, I wrote,
To navigate that lot without a bone broke.

And don't you dare venture to College Green
To have a chinwag with the OLD Queen,
'Cos you'll take your life in your hands up there
With skateboarders crashing about everywhere.
And the Cathedral's no place for a Royal to hide,
'Cos they'm doin' their tricks down the aisles inside.

And if Philip suggests a look round the quays,
Steer him away, Your Majesty, please,
For the Bikers and Boarders have now gained control
Of all that as well, so it's no place to stroll.
And you might trip over a blanket or two
With the Hungry and Homeless forming a queue.

Should the Duke head for Brunel's *Great Britain*
Then turn him back round posthaste,
'Cos what you'll encounter along the way
You'll find in very poor taste.
Benidorm's come to Bristol, you see.
(A right blot on the landscape, between you and me).

But if you should fancy a nice sit down
In that cosmopolitan bit of town,
You won't have to travel very far
For a cappuccino, latte, or char,
'Cos we'm over-run with cafés and bars,
In this culture-bid-seeking-city of ours.

But ... having got that off me chest,
If she DID come, I told her, then I'd suggest
A cruise round The Downs might suit her best,
And I'd guarantee she'd be impressed.
That jewel in our crown would pass any test
'Cos our Planners DAREN'T meddle with Bristol West.

I write to entertain, my dears,
I write not to inform.
I simply write to bring a smile
To those who feel forlorn.
The world today is full of woe,
Misery and pain.
Light-hearted deviation
Is the goal for which I aim.
So waste no time in trying to find
Life's 'hidden meaning' here.
I haven't solved that riddle, yet,
Nor ever will, I fear.